I0164055

Mine Eyes Have Seen

Mine Eyes Have Seen

A Play in One Act

Alice Dunbar Nelson

MINT EDITIONS

Mine Eyes Have Seen: A Play in One Act was first published in 1918.

This edition published by Mint Editions 2021.

ISBN 9781513282459 | E-ISBN 9781513287478

Published by Mint Editions®

MINT
EDITIONS
minteditionbooks.com

Publishing Director: Jennifer Newens
Design & Production: Rachel Lopez Metzger
Project Manager: Micaela Clark
Typesetting: Westchester Publishing Services

CHARACTERS

DAN: the cripple
CHRIS: the younger brother
LUCY: the sister
MRS. O'NEILL: an Irish neighbor
JAKE: a Jewish boy
JULIA: Chris' sweetheart
BILL HARVEY: a muleteer
CORNELIA LEWIS: a settlement worker

Time: Now (1918)
Place: A manufacturing city in the northern part
of the United States.

(*Kitchen of a tenement. All details of furnishing emphasize sordidness—laundry tubs, range, table covered with oil cloth, pine chairs. Curtain discloses Dan in a rude imitation of a steamer chair, propped by faded pillows, his feet covered with a patch-work quilt*)

(*Lucy is bustling about the range preparing a meal. During the conversation she moves from range to table, setting latter and making ready the noon-day meal*)

(*Dan is about thirty years old; face thin, pinched, bearing traces of suffering. His hair is prematurely grey; nose finely chiselled; eyes wide, as if seeing* BEYOND. *Complexion brown*)

(*Lucy is slight, frail, brown-skinned, about twenty, with a pathetic face. She walks with a slight limp*)

DAN: Isn't it most time for him to come home, Lucy?

LUCY: It's hard to tell, Danny, dear; Chris doesn't come home on time anymore. It's half-past twelve, and he ought to be here by the clock, but you can't tell any more—you can't tell.

DAN: Where does he go?

LUCY: I know where he doesn't go, Dan, but where he does, I can't say. He's not going to Julia's any more lately. I'm afraid, Dan, I'm afraid!

DAN: Of what, Little Sister?

LUCY: Of everything; oh, Dan, it's too big, too much for me—the world outside, the street—Chris going and coming home nights moody-eyed; I don't understand.

DAN: And so you're afraid? That's been the trouble from the beginning of time—we're afraid because we don't understand.

LUCY: (*coming down front, with a dish cloth in her hand*) Oh, Dan, wasn't it better in the old days when we were back home—in the little house with the garden, and you and father coming home nights and mother getting supper, and Chris and I studying lessons in the dining-room at the table—we didn't have to eat and live in the kitchen then, and—

DAN: (*grimly*)—And the notices posted on the fence for us to leave town because niggers had no business having such a decent home.

LUCY: (*unheeding the interruption*)—And Chris and I reading the wonderful books and laying our plans—

DAN: —To see them go up in the smoke of our burned home.

LUCY: (*continuing, her back to Dan, her eyes lifted, as if seeing a vision of retrospect*)—And everyone petting me because I had hurt my foot when I was little, and father—

DAN: —Shot down like a dog for daring to defend his home—

LUCY: —Calling me "Little Brown Princess," and telling mother—

DAN: —Dead of pneumonia and heartbreak in this bleak climate.

LUCY: —That when you—

DAN: —Maimed for life in a factory of hell! Useless—useless—broken on the wheel.

(*His voice breaks in a dry sob*)

LUCY: (*Coming out of her trance, she throws aside the dish-cloth, and running to Dan, lays her cheek against his and strokes his hair*) Poor Danny, poor Danny, forgive me, I'm selfish.

DAN: Not selfish, Little Sister, merely natural.

(*Enter roughly and unceremoniously Chris. He glances at the two with their arms about each other, shrugs his shoulders, hangs up his rough cap and mackinaw on a nail, then seats himself at the table, his shoulders hunched up; his face dropping on his hand. Lucy approaches him timidly*)

LUCY: Tired, Chris?

CHRIS: No.

LUCY: Ready for dinner?

CHRIS: If it's ready for me.

LUCY: (*busies herself bringing dishes to the table*) You're late today.

CHRIS: I have bad news. My number was posted today.

LUCY: Number? Posted?

(*Pauses with a plate in her hand*)

CHRIS: I'm drafted.

LUCY: (*Drops plate with a crash. Dan leans forward tensely, his hands grasping the arms of his chair*) Oh, it can't be! They won't take you from us! And shoot you down, too? What will Dan do?

DAN: Never mind about me, Sister. And you're drafted, boy?

CHRIS: Yes—yes—but—(*He rises and strikes the table heavily with his hand*) I'm not going.

DAN: Your duty—

CHRIS: —Is here with you. I owe none elsewhere, I'll pay none.

LUCY: Chris! Treason! I'm afraid!

CHRIS: Yes, of course, you're afraid, Little Sister, why shouldn't you be? Haven't you had your soul shrivelled with fear since we were driven like dogs from our home? And for what? Because we were living like Christians. Must I go and fight for the nation that let my father's murder go unpunished? That killed my mother—that took away my chances for making a man out of myself? Look at us—you—Dan, a shell of a man—

DAN: Useless—useless—

LUCY: Hush, Chris!

CHRIS: —And me, with a fragment of an education, and no chance— only half a man. And you, poor Little Sister, there's no chance for you; what is there in life for you? No, if others want to fight, let them. I'll claim exemption.

DAN: On what grounds?

CHRIS: You—and Sister. I am all you have; I support you.

DAN: (*half rising in his chair*) Hush! Have I come to this, that I should be the excuse, the woman's skirts for a slacker to hide behind?

CHRIS: (*clenching his fists*) You call me that? You, whom I'd lay down my life for? I'm no slacker when I hear the real call of duty. Shall I desert the cause that needs me—you—Sister—home? For a fancied glory? Am I to take up the cause of a lot of kings and politicians who play with men's souls, as if they are cards— dealing them out, a hand here, in the Somme—a hand there, in Palestine—a hand there, in the Alps—a hand there, in Russia— and because the cards don't match well, call it a misdeal, gather them up, throw them in the discard, and call for a new deal of a million human, suffering souls? And I must be the Deuce of Spades?

(*During the speech, the door opens slowly and Jake lounges in. He is a slight, pale youth, Hebraic, thin-lipped, eager-eyed. His hands are in his pockets, his narrow shoulders drawn forward. At the end of Chris' speech he applauds softly*)

JAKE: Bravo! You've learned the patter well. Talk like the fellows at the Socialist meetings.

DAN and LUCY: Socialist meetings!

CHRIS: (*defiantly*) Well?

DAN: Oh, nothing; it explains. All right, go on—any more?

JAKE: Guess he's said all he's got breath for. I'll go; it's too muggy in here. What's the row?

CHRIS: I'm drafted.

JAKE: Get exempt. Easy—if you don't want to go. As for me—

(*Door opens, and Mrs. O'Neill bustles in. She is in deep mourning, plump, Irish, shrewd-looking, bright-eyed*)

MRS. O'NEILL: Lucy, they do be sayin' as how down by the chain stores they be a raid on the potatoes, an' ef ye'er wantin' some, ye'd better be after gittin' into yer things an' comin' wid me. I kin kape the crowd off yer game foot—an' what's the matter wid youse all?

LUCY: Oh, Mrs. O'Neill, Chris has got to go to war.

MRS. O'NEILL: An' ef he has, what of it? Ye'll starve, that's all.

DAN: Starve? Never! He'll go, we'll live.

(*Lucy wrings her hands impotently. Mrs. O'Neill drops a protecting arm about the girl's shoulder*)

MRS. O'NEILL: An' it's hard it seems to yer? But they took me man from me year before last, an' he wint afore I came over here, an' it's a widder I am wid me five kiddies, an' I've niver a word to say but—

CHRIS: He went to fight for his own. What do they do for my people? They don't want us, except in extremity. They treat us like—like—like—

JAKE: Like Jews in Russia, eh?

(*He slouches forward, then his frame straightens itself electrically*)

Like Jews in Russia, eh? Denied the right of honor in men, eh? Or the right of virtue in women, eh? There isn't a wrong you can name that your race has endured that mine has not suffered, too. But there's a future, Chris—a big one. We younger ones must be in that future—ready for it, ready for it—

(*His voice trails off, and he sinks despondently into a chair*)

CHRIS: Future? Where? Not in this country? Where?

(*The door opens and Julia rushes in impulsively. She is small, slightly built, eager-eyed, light-brown skin, wealth of black hair; full of sudden shyness*)

JULIA: Oh, Chris, someone has just told me—I was passing by—one of the girls said your number was called. Oh, Chris, will you have to go?

(*She puts her arms up to Chris' neck; he removes them gently, and makes a slight gesture toward Dan's chair*)

JULIA: Oh, I forgot. Dan, excuse me. Lucy, it's terrible, isn't it?

CHRIS: I'm not going, Julia.

MRS. O'NEILL: Not going!

DAN: Our men have always gone, Chris. They went in 1776.

CHRIS: Yes, as slaves. Promised a freedom they never got.

DAN: No, gladly, and saved the day, too, many a time. Ours was the first blood shed on the altar of National liberty. We went in 1812, on land and sea. Our men were through the struggles of 1861—

CHRIS: When the Nation was afraid not to call them. Didn't want 'em at first.

DAN: Never mind; they helped work out their own salvation. And they were there in 1898—

CHRIS: Only to have their valor disputed.

DAN: —And they were at Carrizal, my boy, and now—

MRS. O'NEILL: An' sure, wid a record like that—ah, 'tis me ould man who said at first 'twasn't his quarrel. His Oireland bled an' the work of thim divils to try to make him a traitor nearly broke his heart—but he said he'd go to do his bit—an' here I am.

(*There is a sound of noise and bustle without, and with a loud laugh, Bill Harvey enters. He is big, muscular, rough, his voice thunderous. He emits cries of joy at seeing the group, shakes hands and claps Chris and Dan on their backs*)

DAN: And so you weren't torpedoed?

HARVEY: No, I'm here for a while—to get more mules and carry them to the front to kick their bit.

MRS. O'NEILL: You've been—over there?

HARVEY: Yes, over the top, too. Mules, rough-necks, wires, mud, dead bodies, stench, terror!

JULIA: (*horror-stricken*) Ah—Chris!

CHRIS: Never, mind, not for mine.

HARVEY: It's a great life—not. But I'm off again, first chance.

MRS. O'NEILL: They're brutes, eh?

HARVEY: Don't remind me.

MRS. O'NEILL: (*whispering*) They maimed my man, before he died.

JULIA: (*clinging to Chris*) Not you, oh, not you!

HARVEY: They crucified children.

DAN: Little children? They crucified little children.

CHRIS: Well, what's that to us? They're little white children. But here our fellow countrymen throw our little black babies in the flames—as did the worshippers of Moloch, only they haven't the excuse of a religious rite.

JAKE: (*slouches out of his chair, in which he has been sitting brooding*) Say, don't you get tired sitting around grieving because you're colored? I'd be ashamed to be—

DAN: Stop! Who's ashamed of his race? Ours the glorious inheritance; ours the price of achievement. Ashamed! I'm proud. And you, too, Chris, smouldering in youthful wrath, you, too, are proud to be numbered with the darker ones, soon to come into their inheritance.

MRS. O'NEILL: Aye, but you've got to fight to keep yer inheritance. Ye can't lay down when someone else has done the work, and expect it to go on. Ye've got to fight.

JAKE: If you're proud, show it. All of your people—well, look at us! Is there a greater race than ours? Have any people had more horrible persecutions—and yet—we're loyal always to the country where we live and serve.

MRS. O'NEILL: And us! Look at us!

DAN: (*half tears himself from the chair, the upper part of his body writhing, while the lower part is inert, dead*) Oh, God! If I were but whole and strong! If I could only prove to a doubting world of what stuff my people are made!

JULIA: But why, Dan, it isn't our quarrel? What have we to do with their affairs? These white people, they hate us. Only today I was sneered at when I went to help with some of their relief work. Why should you, my Chris, go to help those who hate you?

(*Chris clasps her in his arms, and they stand, defying the others*)

HARVEY: If you could have seen the babies and girls—and old women—if you could have—

(*Covers his eyes with his hand*)

CHRIS: Well, it's good for things to be evened up somewhere.

DAN: Hush, Chris! It is not for us to visit retribution. Nor to wish hatred on others. Let us rather remember the good that has come to us. Love of humanity is above the small considerations of time or place or race or sect. Can't you be big enough to feel pity for the little crucified French children—for the ravished Polish girls, even as their mothers must have felt sorrow, if they had known, for our burned and maimed little ones? Oh, Mothers of Europe, we be of one blood, you and I!

(*There is a tense silence. Julia turns from Chris, and drops her hand. He moves slowly to the window and looks out. The door opens quietly, and Cornelia Lewis comes in. She stands still a moment, as if sensing a difficult situation*)

CORNELIA: I've heard about it, Chris, your country calls you.

(*Chris turns from the window and waves hopeless hands at Dan and Lucy*)

Yes, I understand; they do need you, don't they?

DAN: (*fiercely*) No!

ALICE DUNBAR NELSON

LUCY: Yes, we do, Chris, we do need you, but your country needs you more. And, above that, your race is calling you to carry on its good name, and with that, the voice of humanity is calling to us all—we can manage without you, Chris.

CHRIS: You? Poor little crippled Sister. Poor Dan—

DAN: Don't pity me, pity your poor, weak self.

CHRIS: (*clenching his fist*) Brother, you've called me two names today that no man ought to have to take—a slacker and a weakling!

DAN: True. Aren't you both?

(*Leans back and looks at Chris speculatively*)

CHRIS: (*Makes an angry lunge towards the chair, then flings his hands above his head in an impatient gesture*)

Oh, God!

(*Turns back to the window*)

JULIA: Chris, it's wicked for them to taunt you so—but Chris—it is our country—our race—

(*Outside the strains of music from a passing band are heard. The music comes faintly, gradually growing louder and louder until it reaches a crescendo. The tune is "The Battle Hymn of the Republic," played in stirring march time*)

DAN: (*singing softly*) "Mine eyes have seen the glory of the coming of the Lord!"

CHRIS: (*turns from the window and straightens his shoulders*) And Mine!

CORNELIA: "As he died to make men holy, let us die to make them free!"

MRS. O'NEILL: An' ye'll make the sacrifice, me boy, an' ye'll be the happier.

JAKE: Sacrifice! No sacrifice for him, it's those who stay behind. Ah, if they would only call me, and call me soon!

LUCY: We'll get on, never fear. I'm proud! Proud!

(*Her voice breaks a little, but her head is thrown back*)

(*As the music draws nearer, the group breaks up, and the whole roomful rushes to the window and looks out. Chris remains in the center of the floor, rigidly at attention, a rapt look on his face. Dan strains at his chair, as if he would rise, then sinks back, his hand feebly beating time to the music, which swells to a martial crash*)

CURTAIN

A Note About the Author

Alice Dunbar Nelson (1875–1935) was an African American poet, journalist, and political activist. Born in New Orleans to a formerly enslaved seamstress and a white seaman, Dunbar Nelson was raised in the city's traditional Creole community. In 1892, she graduated from Straight University and began working as a teacher in the New Orleans public school system. In 1895, having published her debut collection of poems and short stories, she moved to New York City, where she cofounded the White Rose Mission in Manhattan. Dunbar Nelson married poet Paul Laurence Dunbar in 1898 after several years of courtship, but their union soon proved abusive. She separated from Dunbar—whose violence and alcoholism had become intolerable—in 1902, after which Nelson taught at Howard High School in Wilmington, Delaware for around a decade. She continued to write and earned a reputation as a passionate activist for equality and the end of racial violence. Her one-act play *My Eyes Have Seen* (1918) was published in *The Crisis*, the journal of the NAACP. Dunbar Nelson settled in Philadelphia in 1932 with her third husband Robert J. Nelson and remained in the city until her death. Her career is exemplified by a mastery of literary forms—in her journalism, stories, plays, and poems, she made a place for herself in the male-dominated world of the Harlem Renaissance while remaining true to her vision of political change and social uplift for all African Americans.

A Note from the Publisher

Spanning many genres, from non-fiction essays to literature classics to children's books and lyric poetry, Mint Edition books showcase the master works of our time in a modern new package. The text is freshly typeset, is clean and easy to read, and features a new note about the author in each volume. Many books also include exclusive new introductory material. Every book boasts a striking new cover, which makes it as appropriate for collecting as it is for gift giving. Mint Edition books are only printed when a reader orders them, so natural resources are not wasted. We're proud that our books are never manufactured in excess and exist only in the exact quantity they need to be read and enjoyed.

bookfinity™

Discover more of your favorite classics with Bookfinity™.

- Track your reading with custom book lists.
- Get great book recommendations for your personalized Reader Type.
- Add reviews for your favorite books.
- AND MUCH MORE!

Visit **bookfinity.com** and take the fun Reader Type quiz to get started.

Enjoy our classic and modern companion pairings!

Classic & Modern

Bookfinity is a registered trademark of Ingram Book Group LLC. © 2023 Bookfinity. All rights reserved.

www.ingramcontent.com/pod-product-compliance
Lightning Source LLC
Chambersburg PA
CBHW020451030426
42337CB00014B/1503